THOMAS GRAY

Selected
Poems

BLOOMSBURY
* POETRY *
CLASSICS

This selection by Ian Hamilton
first published 1997
Copyright © 1997 by Bloomsbury Publishing Plc
Bloomsbury Publishing Plc, 38 Soho Square,
London WIV 5DF

A CIP catalogue record for this book
is available from the British Library

ISBN 0 7475 3732 1

10 9 8 7 6 5 4 3 2 1

Typeset in Great Britain by
Hewer Text Composition Services, Edinburgh
Printed in Great Britain by St Edmundsbury Press, Suffolk
Jacket design by Jeff Fisher

CONTENTS

ODE ON THE SPRING

Lo! where the rosy-bosomed Hours,
    Fair Venus' train, appear,
Disclose the long-expecting flowers
    And wake the purple year!
The Attic warbler pours her throat
Responsive to the cuckoo's note,
The untaught harmony of Spring:
    While, whispering pleasure as they fly,
    Cool Zephyrs through the clear blue sky
Their gathered fragrance fling.

Where'er the oak's thick branches stretch
    A broader, browner shade,
Where'er the rude and moss-grown beech
    O'er-canopies the glade,
Beside some water's rushy brink
With me the Muse shall sit, and think
(At ease reclined in rustic state)
    How vain the ardour of the Crowd;
    How low, how little are the Proud,
How indigent the Great!

Still is the toiling hand of Care;
    The panting herds repose:
Yet hark, how through the peopled air
    The busy murmur glows!
The insect youth are on the wing,
Eager to taste the honied spring
And float amid the liquid noon:
    Some lightly o'er the current skim,
    Some show their gaily-gilded trim
Quick-glancing to the sun.

To Contemplation's sober eye
    Such is the race of Man:
And they that creep, and they that fly,
    Shall end where they began.
Alike the busy and the gay
But flutter through life's little day,
In Fortune's varying colours dressed:
    Brushed by the hand of rough Mischance,
    Or chilled by Age, their airy dance
    They leave, in dust to rest.

Methinks I hear in accents low
    The sportive kind reply:
Poor moralist! and what art thou?
    A solitary fly!
Thy joys no glittering female meets,
No hive hast thou of hoarded sweets,
No painted plumage to display:
    On hasty wings thy youth is flown;
    Thy sun is set, thy spring is gone –
We frolic while 'tis May.

ODE ON A DISTANT
PROSPECT OF ETON COLLEGE

Ye distant spires, ye antique towers
  That crown the watery glade,
Where grateful Science still adores
  Her Henry's holy shade;
And ye, that from the stately brow
Of Windsor's heights th' expanse below
  Of grove, of lawn, of mead survey,
Whose turf, whose shade, whose flowers among
Wanders the hoary Thames along
  His silver-winding way:

Ah happy hills! ah pleasing shade!
  Ah fields beloved in vain!
Where once my careless childhood strayed,
  A stranger yet to pain!
I feel the gales that from ye blow
A momentary bliss bestow,
  As waving fresh their gladsome wing
My weary soul they seem to soothe,
And, redolent of joy and youth,
  To breathe a second spring.

Say, Father Thames, for thou hast seen
    Full many a sprightly race
Disporting on thy margent green
    The paths of pleasure trace;
Who foremost now delight to cleave
With pliant arm, thy glassy wave?
    The captive linnet which enthral?
What idle progeny succeed
To chase the rolling circle's speed
    Or urge the flying ball?

While some on earnest business bent
    Their murmuring labours ply
'Gainst graver hours, that bring constraint
    To sweeten liberty:
Some bold adventurers disdain
The limits of their little reign
    And unknown regions dare descry:
Still as they run they look behind,
They hear a voice in every wind,
    And snatch a fearful joy.

Gay hope is theirs by fancy fed,
    Less pleasing when possest;
The tear forgot as soon as shed,
    The sunshine of the breast:
Theirs buxom health, of rosy hue,
Wild wit, invention ever new,
    And lively cheer, of vigour born;
The thoughtless day, the easy night,
The spirits pure, the slumbers light
    That fly th' approach of morn.

Alas! regardless of their doom
    The little victims play!
No sense have they of ills to come
    Nor care beyond to-day:
Yet see how all around them wait
The Ministers of human fate
    And black Misfortune's baleful train!
Ah show them where in ambush stand
To seize their prey, the murderous band!
    Ah, tell them they are men!

These shall the fury Passions tear,
    The vultures of the mind,
Disdainful Anger, pallid Fear,
    And Shame that skulks behind,
Or pining Love shall waste their youth;
Or Jealousy with rankling tooth
    That inly gnaws the secret heart,
And Envy wan, and faded Care,
Grim-visaged comfortless Despair,
    And Sorrow's piercing dart.

Ambition this shall tempt to rise,
    Then whirl the wretch from high,
To bitter Scorn a sacrifice
    And grinning Infamy.
The stings of Falsehood those shall try,
And hard Unkindness' altered eye,
    That mocks the tear it forced to flow;
And keen Remorse with blood defiled,
And moody Madness laughing wild
    Amid severest woe.

Lo, in the vale of years beneath
    A griesly troop are seen,
The painful family of Death,
    More hideous than their Queen:
This racks the joints, this fires the veins,
That every labouring sinew strains,
    Those in the deeper vitals rage:
Lo, Poverty, to fill the band,
That numbs the soul with icy hand,
    And slow-consuming Age.

To each his sufferings: all are men;
    Condemned alike to groan;
The tender for another's pain,
    Th' unfeeling for his own.
Yet, ah! why should they know their fate,
Since sorrow never comes too late,
    And happiness too swiftly flies?
Thought would destroy their paradise.
No more; – where ignorance is bliss,
    'Tis folly to be wise.

AMATORY LINES

With beauty, with pleasure surrounded, to languish –
To weep without knowing the cause of my anguish:
To start from short slumbers, and wish for the
   morning –
To close my dull eyes when I see it returning;
Sighs sudden and frequent, looks dejected –
Words that steal from my tongue, by no meaning
   connected!
Ah, say, fellow-swains, how these symptoms befell me?
They smile, but reply not – Sure Delia will tell me!

SONG

Thyrsis, when we parted, swore
   Ere the spring he would return –
Ah! what means you violet flower!
   And the bud that decks the thorn!
'Twas the lark that upward sprung!
'Twas the nightingale that sung!

Idle notes! untimely green!
   Why this unavailing haste?
Western gales and skies serene
   Speak not always winter past.
Cease, my doubts, my fears to move,
Spare the honour of my love.

HYMN TO ADVERSITY

Daughter of Jove, relentless power,
    Thou tamer of the human breast,
Whose iron scourge and torturing hour
    The bad affright, afflict the best!
Bound in thy admantine chain
The proud are taught to taste of pain,
And purple tyrants vainly groan
With pangs unfelt before, unpitied and alone.

When first thy Sire to send on earth
    Virtue, his darling child, designed,
To thee he gave the heavenly birth
    And bade to form her infant mind.
Stern, rugged Nurse! thy rigid lore
With patience many a year she bore:
What sorrow was, thou bad'st her know,
And from her own she learned to melt at others' woe.

Scared at thy frown terrific, fly
    Self-pleasing Folly's idle brood,
Wild Laughter, Noise, and thoughtless Joy,
    And leave us leisure to be good.
Light they disperse, and with them go
The summer Friend, the flattering Foe;
    By vain Prosperity received,
To her they vow their truth, and are again believed.

Wisdom in sable garb arrayed
    Immersed in rapturous thought profound,
And Melancholy, silent maid,
    With leaden eye, that loves the ground,
Still on thy solemn steps attend;
Warm Charity, the general friend,
    With Justice, to herself severe,
And Pity dropping soft the sadly-pleasing tear.

O, gently on thy suppliant's head,
    Dread Goddess, lay thy chastening hand!
Not in thy Gorgon terrors clad,
    Nor circled with the vengeful band
(As by the impious thou art seen)
With thundering voice, and threatening mien,
    With screaming Horror's funeral cry,
Despair, and fell Disease, and ghastly Poverty;

Thy form benign, O Goddess, wear,
    Thy milder influence impart,
Thy philosophic train be there
    To soften, not to wound my heart.
The generous spark extinct revive,
Teach me to love and to forgive,
    Teach my own defects to scan,
What others are to feel, and know myself a Man.

TOPHET

Such Tophet was; so looked the grinning fiend
Whom many a frighted prelate called his friend;
I saw them bow and, while they wished him dead,
With servile simper nod the mitred head.
Our Mother-Church with half-averted sight
Blushed as she blessed her grisly proselyte:
Hosannahs rung through hell's tremendous borders,
And Satan's self had thoughts of taking orders.

ON A FAVOURITE CAT, DROWNED IN A TUB OF
GOLD FISHES

'Twas on a lofty vase's side,
Where China's gayest art had dyed
   The azure flowers that blow;
Demurest of the tabby kind,
The pensive Selima reclined,
   Gazed on the lake below.

Her conscious tail her joy declared;
The fair round face, the snowy beard,
   The velvet of her paws,
Her coat, that with the tortoise vies,
Her ears of jet, and emerald eyes,
   She saw; and purred applause.

Still had she gazed; but 'midst the tide
Two angel forms were seen to glide,
   The Genii of the stream:
Their scaly armour's Tyrian hue
Through richest purple to the view
   Betrayed a golden gleam.

The hapless Nymph with wonder saw:
A whisker first and then a claw,
   With many an ardent wish,
She stretched in vain to reach the prize.
What female heart can gold despise?
   What Cat's averse to fish?

Presumptuous Maid! with looks intent
Again she stretched, again she bent,
    Nor knew the gulf between.
(Malignant Fate sat by, and smiled.)
The slipp'ry verge her feet beguiled,
    She tumbled headlong in.

Eight times emerging from the flood
She mewed to every watery god,
    Some speedy aid to send.
No Dolphin came, no Nereid stirred:
Nor cruel *Tom*, nor *Susan* heard.
    A Fav'rite has no friend!

From hence, ye Beauties, undeceived,
Know, one false step is ne'er retrieved,
    And be with caution bold.
Not all that tempts your wand'ring eyes
And heedless hearts, is lawful prize;
    Nor all that glisters, gold.

ELEGY WRITTEN IN A COUNTRY CHURCHYARD

The curfew tolls the knell of parting day,
  The lowing herd winds slowly o'er the lea,
The plowman homeward plods his weary way,
  And leaves the world to darkness and to me.

Now fades the glimmering landscape on the sight,
  And all the air a solemn stillness holds,
Save where the beetle wheels his droning flight,
  And drowsy tinklings lull the distant folds;

Save that from yonder ivy-mantled tower
  The moping owl does to the moon complain
Of such as, wand'ring near her secret bower,
  Molest her ancient solitary reign.

Beneath those rugged elms, that yew-tree's shade,
  Where heaves the turf in many a mould'ring heap,
Each in his narrow cell for ever laid,
  The rude forefathers of the hamlet sleep.

The breezy call of incense-breathing morn,
  The swallow twitt'ring from the straw-built shed,
The cock's shrill clarion, or the echoing horn,
  No more shall rouse them from their lowly bed.

For them no more the blazing hearth shall burn,
    Or busy housewife ply her evening care:
No children run to lisp their sire's return,
    Or climb his knees the envied kiss to share.

Oft did the harvest to their sickle yield,
    Their furrow oft the stubborn glebe has broke:
How jocund did they drive their team afield!
    How bowed the woods beneath their sturdy stroke!

Let not Ambition mock their useful toil,
    Their homely joys, and destiny obscure;
Nor Grandeur hear with a disdainful smile
    The short and simple annals of the poor.

The boast of heraldry, the pomp of power,
    And all that beauty, all that wealth e'er gave,
Awaits alike th' inevitable hour:
    The paths of glory lead but to the grave.

Nor you, ye proud, impute to These the fault,
    If Memory o'er their tomb no trophies raise,
Where through the long-drawn aisle and fretted vault
    The pealing anthem swells the note of praise.

Can storied urn or animated bust
    Back to its mansion call the fleeting breath?
Can Honour's voice provoke the silent dust,
    Or Flatt'ry soothe the dull cold ear of death?

Perhaps in this neglected spot is laid
    Some heart once pregnant with celestial fire;
Hands, that the rod of empire might have swayed,
    Or waked to ecstasy the living lyre.

But Knowledge to their eyes her ample page
    Rich with the spoils of time did ne'er unroll;
Chill Penury repressed their noble rage,
    And froze the genial current of the soul.

Full many a gem of purest ray serene
    The dark unfathomed caves of ocean bear;
Full many a flower is born to blush unseen,
    And waste its sweetness on the desert air.

Some village Hampden that with dauntless breast
    The little tyrant of his fields withstood,
Some mute inglorious Milton here may rest,
    Some Cromwell guiltless of his country's blood.

Th' applause of list'ning senates to command,
  The threats of pain and ruin to despise,
To scatter plenty o'er a smiling land,
  And read their history in a nation's eyes,

Their lot forbade: nor circumscribed alone
  Their growing virtues, but their crimes confined;
Forbade to wade through slaughter to a throne,
  And shut the gates of mercy on mankind,

The struggling pangs of conscious truth to hide,
  To quench the blushes of ingenuous shame,
Or heap the shrine of Luxury and Pride
  With incense kindled at the Muse's flame.

Far from the madding crowd's ignoble strife
  Their sober wishes never learned to stray;
Along the cool sequestered vale of life.
  They kept the noiseless tenor of their way.

Yet ev'n these bones from insult to protect
  Some frail memorial still erected nigh,
With uncouth rhymes and shapeless sculpture decked,
  Implores the passing tribute of a sigh.

Their name, their years, spelt by th' unlettered Muse,
 The place of fame and elegy supply:
And many a holy text around she strews,
 That teach the rustic moralist to die.

For who, to dumb Forgetfulness a prey,
 This pleasing anxious being e'er resigned,
Left the warm precincts of the cheerful day,
 Nor cast one longing ling'ring look behind?

On some fond breast the parting soul relies,
 Some pious drops the closing eye requires;
E'en from the tomb the voice of Nature cries,
 E'en in our Ashes live their wonted fires.

For thee, who, mindful of th' unhonoured dead,
 Dost in these lines their artless tale relate;
If chance, by lonely contemplation led,
 Some kindred spirit shall inquire thy fate,

Haply some hoary-headed Swain may say,
 'Oft have we seen him at the peep of dawn
Brushing with hasty steps the dews away
 To meet the sun upon the upland lawn.

'There at the foot of yonder nodding beech
   That wreathes its old fantastic roots so high,
His listless length at noontide would he stretch,
   And pore upon the brook that babbles by.

'Hard by yon wood, now smiling as in scorn,
   Mutt'ring his wayward fancies he would rove,
Now drooping, woeful wan, like one forlorn,
   Or crazed with care, or crossed in hopeless love.

'One morn I missed him on the customed hill,
   Along the heath and near his fav'rite tree;
Another came; nor yet beside the rill,
   Nor up the lawn, nor at the wood was he;

'The next with dirges due in sad array
   Slow through the church-way path we saw him borne.
Approach and read (for thou canst read) the lay
   Graved on the stone beneath yon aged thorn:'

The Epitaph

Here rests his head upon the lap of Earth
   A Youth to Fortune and to Fame unknown.
Fair Science frowned not on his humble birth,
   And Melancholy marked him for her own.

Large was his bounty, and his soul sincere,
   Heaven did a recompense as largely send:
He gave to Mis'ry all he had, a tear,
   He gained from Heaven ('twas all he wished) a friend.

No further seek his merits to disclose,
   Or draw his frailties from their dread abode,
(There they alike in trembling hope respose,)
   The bosom, of his Father and his God.

SONNET ON THE DEATH OF MR RICHARD WEST

In vain to me the smiling mornings shine,
    And redd'ning Phoebus lifts his golden fire:
The birds in vain their amorous descant join;
    Or cheerful fields resume their green attire:
These ears, alas! for other notes repine
    A different object do these eyes require:
My lonely anguish melts no heart but mine;
    And in my breast the imperfect joys expire.
Yet morning smiles the busy race to cheer,
    And new-born pleasure brings to happier men:
The fields to all their wonted tribute bear:
    To warm their little loves the birds complain:
I fruitless mourn to him that cannot hear,
    And weep the more, because I weep in vain.

A LONG STORY

In Britain's isle, no matter where,
    An ancient pile of building stands:
The Huntingdons and Hattons there
    Employ'd the pow'r of fairy hands

To raise the ceiling's fretted height,
    Each pannel in achievements clothing,
Rich windows that exclude the light,
    And passages, that lead to nothing.

Full oft within the spacious walls,
    When he had fifty winters o'er him,
My grave Lord-Keeper led the brawls;
    The seals and maces danc'd before him.

His bushy bread, and shoe-strings green,
    His high-crown'd hat, and satin doublet,
Mov'd the stout heart of England's queen,
    Though Pope and Spaniard could not trouble it.

What, in the very first beginning!
   Shame of the versifying tribe!
Your hist'ry whither are you spinning!
   Can you do nothing but describe?

A house there is (and that's enough)
   From whence one fatal morning issues
A brace of warriors, not in buff,
   But rustling in their silks and tissues.

The first came cap-a-pee from France,
   Her conqu'ring destiny fulfilling,
Whom meaner beauties eye askance,
   And vainly ape her art of killing.

The other amazon kind heav'n
   Had arm'd with spirit, wit, and satire;
But Cobham had the polish giv'n,
   And tipp'd her arrows with good-nature.

To celebrate her eyes, her air–
   Coarse panegyrics would but tease her;
Melissa is her 'nom de guerre.'
   Alas, who would not wish to please her!

With bonnet blue and capuchine,
    And aprons long, they hid their armour;
And veil'd their weapons, bright and keen,
    In pity to the country farmer.

Fame, in the shape of Mr P – t
    (By this time all the parish know it),
Had told that thereabouts there lurk'd
    A wicked imp they call a poet:

Who prowl'd the country far and near,
    Bewitch'd the children of the peasants,
Dried up the cows, and lam'd the deer,
    And suck'd the eggs, and kill'd the pheasants.

My lady heard their joint petition,
    Swore by her coronet and ermine,
She'd issue out her high commission
    To rid the manor of such vermin.

The heroines undertook the task,
    Thro' lanes unknown, o'er stiles they ventur'd,
Rapp'd at the door, nor stay'd to ask,
    But bounce into the parlour enter'd.

The trembling family they daunt,
    They flirt, they sing, they laugh, they tattle,
Rummage his mother, pinch his aunt,
    And upstairs in a whirlwind rattle:

Each hole and cupboard they explore,
    Each creek and cranny of his chamber,
Run hurry-scurry round the floor,
    And o'er the bed and tester clamber;

Into the drawers and china pry,
    Papers and books, a huge imbroglio!
Under a tea-cup he might lie,
    Or creased, like dog-ears, in a folio.

On the first marching of the troops,
    The Muses, hopeless of his pardon,
Convey'd him underneath their hoops
    To a small closet in the garden.

So rumour says (who will, believe);
    But that they left the door ajar,
Where, safe and laughing in his sleeve,
    He heard the distant din of war.

Short was his joy. He little knew
　　The pow'r of magic was no fable;
Out of the window, wisk, they flew,
　　But left a spell upon the table.

The words too eager to unriddle,
　　The poet felt a strange disorder;
Transparent bird-lime form'd the middle,
　　And chains invisible the border.

So cunning was the apparatus,
　　The powerful pot-hooks did so move him,
That, will he, nill he, to the great house
　　He went, as if the devil drove him.

Yet on his way (no sign of grace,
　　For folks in fear are apt to pray)
To Phoebus he preferr'd his case,
　　And begg'd his aid that dreadful day.

The godhead would have back'd his quarrel;
　　But with a blush, on recollection,
Own'd that his quiver and his laurel
　　'Gainst four such eyes were no protection.

The court was sate, the culprit there,
    Forth from their gloomy mansions creeping
The lady Janes and Joans repair,
    And from the gallery stand peeping:

Such as in silence of the night
    Come (sweep) along some winding entry
(Styack has often seen the sight),
    Or at the chapel-door stand sentry:

In peaked hoods and mantles tarnish'd,
    Sour visages, enough to scare ye,
High dames of honour once, that garnish'd
    The drawing-room of fierce Queen Mary.

The peeress comes. The audience stare,
    And doff their hats with due submission:
She curtsies, as she takes her chair,
    To all the people of condition.

The bard, with many an artful fib,
    Had in imagination fenc'd him,
Disprov'd the arguments of Squib,
    And all that Groom could urge against him.

But soon his rhetoric forsook him,
    When he the solemn hall had seen;
A sudden fit of ague shook him,
    He stood as mute as poor Macleane.

Yet something he was heard to mutter,
    'How in the park beneath an old tree,
(Without design to hurt the butter
    Or any malice to the poultry),

'He once or twice had penn'd a sonnet;
    Yet hop'd, that he might save his bacon:
Numbers would give their oaths upon it,
    He ne'er was for a conj'rer taken.'

The ghostly prudes with hagged face
    Already had condemn'd the sinner.
My lady rose, and with a grace—
    She smil'd, and bid him come to dinner.

'Jesu-Maria! Madam Bridget,
    Why, what can the Viscountess mean?'
(Cried the square-hoods in woful fidget)
    'The times are alter'd quite and clean!

'Decorum's turn'd to mere civility;
     Her air and all her manners show it.
Commend me to her affability!
     Speak to a commoner and poet!'

     [Heré five hundred stanzas are lost.]

And so God save our noble king,
     And guard us from long-winded lubbers,
That to eternity would sing,
     And keep my lady from her rubbers.

THE PROGRESS OF POESY
A Pindaric Ode

  Awake, Æolian, lyre, awake,
And give to rapture all thy trembling strings,
From Helicon's harmonious springs
  A thousand rills their mazy progress take:
The laughing flowers, that round them blow,
Drink life, and fragrance as they flow.
Now the rich stream of music winds along
Deep, majestic, smooth and strong,
Through verdant vales, and Ceres' golden reign:
Now rolling down the steep amain,
Headlong, impetuous, see it pour;
The rocks and nodding groves rebellow to the roar.

  O Sovereign of the willing soul,
Parent of sweet and solemn-breathing airs,
Enchanting shell! the sullen Cares
  And frantic Passions hear thy soft control.
On Thracia's hills the Lord of War
Has curbed the fury of his car,
And dropped his thirsty lance at thy command.
Perching on the sceptred hand
Of Jove, thy magic lulls the feathered king
With ruffled plumes and flagging wing:
Quenched in dark clouds of slumber lie
The terror of his beak, and lightnings of his eye.

Thee the voice, the dance, obey,
Tempered to thy warbled lay.
    O'er Idalia's velvet-green
    The rosy-crownèd Loves are seen
On Cytherea's day
    With antic Sports, and blue-eyed Pleasures,
    Frisking light in frolic measures;
Now pursuing, now retreating,
    Now in circling troops they meet:
To brisk notes in cadence beating,
    Glance their many-twinkling feet.
Slow melting strains their Queen's approach declare:
    Where'er she turns the Graces homage pay.
With arms sublime, that float upon the air,
    In gliding state she wins her easy way:
O'er her warm cheek and rising bosom move
The bloom of young Desire and purple light of Love.

    Man's feeble race what ills await,
Labour, and Penury, the racks of Pain,
    Disease, and Sorrow's weeping train,
    And Death, sad refuge from the storms of fate!
The fond complaint, my song, disprove,
And justify the laws of Jove.
Say, has he giv'n in vain the heav'nly Muse?
Night, and all her sickly dews,
Her specters wan, and birds of boding cry,
He gives to range the dreary sky:
Till down the eastern cliffs afar
Hyperion's march they spy, and glitt'ring shafts of war.

    In climes beyond the solar road,
Where shaggy forms o'er ice-built mountains roam,
    The Muse has broke the twilight gloom
    To cheer the shiv'ring native's dull abode.
And oft, beneath the odorous shade
Of Chili's boundless forests laid,
She deigns to hear the savage youth repeat
In loose numbers wildly sweet
Their feather-cinctured chiefs, and dusky loves.
Her track, where'er the Goddess roves,
Glory pursue and generous Shame,
Th' unconquerable Mind, and Freedom's holy flame.

Woods, that wave o'er Delphi's steep,
Isles, that crown th' Ægean deep,
   Fields, that cool Ilissus laves,
   Or where Maeander's amber waves
In lingering lab'rinths creep,
   How do your tuneful echoes languish,
   Mute, but to the voice of anguish?
Where each old poetic mountain
   Inspiration breathed around:
Every shade and hallowed fountain
   Murmured deep a solemn sound:
Till the Sad Nine, in Greece's evil hour,
   Left their Parnassus for the Latian plains.
Alike they scorn the pomp of tyrant Power,
   And coward Vice, that revels in her chains.
When Latium had her lofty spirit lost,
They sought, O Albion! next thy sea-encircled coast.

Far from the sun and summer gale,
In thy green lap was Nature's darling laid,
What time, where lucid Avon strayed,
    To him the mighty mother did unveil
Her awful face: the dauntless child
Stretched forth his little arms, and smiled.
This pencil take (she said), whose colours clear
Richly paint the vernal year:
Thine too these golden keys, immortal boy!
This can unlock the gates of joy;
Of horror that, and thrilling fears,
Or ope the sacred source of sympathetic tears.

    Nor second he, that rode sublime
Upon the seraph-wings of Ecstasy,
The secrets of th' abyss to spy.
    He passed the flaming bounds of place and time:
The living throne, the sapphire-blaze,
Where angels tremble while they gaze,
He saw; but blasted with excess of light,
Closed his eyes in endless night.
Behold, where Dryden's less presumptuous car,
Wide o'er the fields of glory bear
Two coursers of ethereal race,
With necks in thunder clothed, and long-resounding
    pace.

Hark, his hands the lyre explore!
Bright-eyed Fancy hovering o'er
 Scatters from her pictured urn
 Thoughts that breathe, and words that burn.
But ah!' tis heard no more –
 O lyre divine! what darling spirit
 Wakes thee now? Though he inherit
Nor the pride, nor ample pinion,
 That the Theban eagle bear
Sailing with supreme dominion
 Through the azure deep of air:
Yet oft before his infant eyes would run
 Such forms as glitter in the Muse's ray,
With orient hues, unborrowed of the sun:
 Yet shall he mount, and keep his distant way
Beyond the limits of a vulgar fate,
Beneath the Good how far – but far above the Great.

THE BARD

A Pindaric Ode

'Ruin seize thee, ruthless King!
  Confusion on thy banners wait!
Though fanned by Conquest's crimson wing
  They mock the air with idle state.
Helm, nor hauberk's twisted mail,
Nor e'en thy virtues, tyrant, shall avail
To save thy secret soul from nightly fears,
From Cambria's curse, from Cambria's tears!'
- Such were the sounds that o'er the crested pride
  Of the first Edward scattered wild dismay,
As down the steep of Snowdon's shaggy side
  He wound with toilsome march his long array:-
Stout Glo'ster stood aghast in speechless trance;
'To arms!' cried Mortimer, and crouched his quivering
    lance.

  On a rock, whose haughty brow
Frowns o'er old Conway's foaming flood,
  Robed in the sable garb of woe,
With haggard eyes the poet stood;
(Loose his beard and hoary hair
Streamed like a meteor to the troubled air;)
And with a master's hand and prophet's fire
Struck the deep sorrows of his lyre:

'Hark, how each giant oak and desert cave
  Sighs to the torrent's awful voice beneath!
O'er thee, O King! their hundred arms they wave
  Revenge on thee in hoarser murmurs breathe;
Vocal no more, since Cambria's fatal day,
To high-born Hoel's harp, or soft Llewellyn's lay.

'Cold is Cadwallo's tongue,
  That hushed the stormy main:
Brave Urien sleeps upon his craggy bed:
  Mountains, ye mourn in vain
  Modred, whose magic song
Made huge Plinlimmon bow his cloud-topt head.
  On dreary Arvon's shore they lie
Smeared with gore and ghastly pale:
Far, far aloof the affrighted ravens sail;
  The famished eagle screams, and passes by.
Dear lost companions of my tuneful art,
  Dear as the light that visits these sad eyes,
Dear as the ruddy drops that warm my heart,
  Ye died amidst your dying country's cries –
No more I weep. They do not sleep;
  On yonder cliffs, a griesly band,
I see them sit; they linger yet,
  Avengers of their native land:
With me in dreadful harmony they join;
And weave with bloody hands the tissue of thy line.

' "Weave the warp and weave the woof,
    The winding-sheet of Edward's race:
Give ample room and verge enough
    The characters of hell to trace.
Mark the year and mark the night
When Severn shall re-echo with affright
The shrieks of death through Berkley's roof that ring,
Shrieks of an agonizing king!
    She-wolf of France, with unrelenting fangs
That tear'st the bowels of thy mangled mate,
    From thee be born, who o'er thy country hangs
The scourge of heaven! What terrors round him wait!
Amazement in his van, with flight combined,
And sorrow's faded form, and solitude behind.

' "Mighty victor, mighty lord,
    Low on his funeral couch he lies!
No pitying heart, no eye, afford
    A tear to grace his obsequies.
Is the sable warrior fled?
Thy son is gone. He rests among the dead.
The swarm that in thy noon-tide beam were born?
– Gone to salute the rising morn.
Fair laughs the morn, and soft the zephyr blows,
    While proudly riding o'er the azure realm
In gallant trim the gilded vessel goes:
    Youth on the prow, and Pleasure at the helm:
Regardless of the sweeping whirlwind's sway,
That, hushed in grim repose, expects his evening prey.

' "Fill high the sparkling bowl,
The rich repast prepare;
    Reft of a crown, he yet may share the feast:
Close by the regal chair
Fell Thirst and Famine scowl
    A baleful smile upon their baffled guest.
Heard ye the din of battle bray,
    Lance to lance, and horse to horse?
    Long years of havoc urge their destined course,
And through the kindred squadrons mow their way.
    Ye towers of Julius, London's lasting shame,
With many a foul and midnight murder fed,
    Revere his consort's faith, his father's fame,
And spare the meek usurper's holy head!
Above, below, the rose of snow,
    Twined with her blushing foe, we spread:
The bristled boar in infant-gore
    Wallows beneath the thorny shade.
Now, brothers, bending o'er the accursèd loom,
Stamp we our vengeance deep, and ratify his doom.

' "Edward, lo! to sudden fate
    (Weave we the woof; The thread is spun;)
Half of thy heart we consecrate.
    (The web is wove; The work is done.)"
Stay, O stay! nor thus forlorn
Leave me unblessed, unpitied, here to mourn:
In yon bright track that fires the western skies
They melt, they vanish from my eyes.

47

But O! what solemn scenes on Snowdon's height
   Descending slow their glittering skirts unroll?
Visions of glory, spare my aching sight,
   Ye unborn ages, crowd not on my soul!
No more our long-lost Arthur we bewail:–
All hail, ye genuine kings! Britannia's issue, hail!

   'Girt with many a baron bold
Sublime their starry fronts they rear;
   And gorgeous dames, and statesmen old
In bearded majesty, appear.
In the midst a form divine!
Her eye proclaims her of the Briton-line:
Her lion-port, her awe-commanding face
Attempered sweet to virgin-grace.
What strings symphonious tremble in the air,
   What strains of vocal transport round her play?
Hear from the grave, great Taliessin, hear;
   They breathe a soul to animate thy clay.
Bright Rapture calls, and soaring as she sings,
Waves in the eye of heaven her many-coloured wings.

   'The verse adorn again
   Fierce war, and faithful love,
And Truth severe, by fairy Fiction drest.
   In buskined measures move
Pale grief, and pleasing pain,
With horror, tyrant of the throbbing breast.

A voice as of the cherub-choir
  Gales from blooming Eden bear,
  And distant warblings lessen on my ear,
That lost in long futurity expire.
Fond impious man, think'st thou yon sanguine cloud
  Raised by thy breath, has quenched the orb of day?
To-morrow he repairs the golden flood
  And warms the nations with redoubled ray.
Enough for me: with joy I see
  The different doom our fates assign:
Be thine despair and sceptred care;
  To triumph and to die are mine.'
– He spoke, and headlong from the mountain's height
Deep in the roaring tide he plunged to endless night.

ODE ON THE PLEASURE ARISING FROM
VICISSITUDE

Now the golden morn aloft
   Waves her dew-bespangled wing,
With vermeil cheek and whisper soft
   She woos the tardy spring:
Till April starts, and calls around
The sleeping fragrance from the ground;
And lightly o'er the living scene
Scatters his freshest, tenderest green.

New-born flocks in rustic dance
   Frisking ply their feeble feet.
Forgetful of their wintry trance
   The birds his presence greet.
But chief, the sky-lark warbles high
His trembling thrilling ecstasy
And, less'ning from the dazzled sight;
Melts into air and liquid light.

Yesterday the sullen year
   Saw the snowy whirlwind fly;
Mute was the music of the air,
   The herd stood drooping by:
Their raptures now that wildly flow,
No yesterday, nor morrow know;
'Tis man alone that joy descries
With forward and reverted eyes.

Smiles on past, Misfortune's brow
   Soft Reflection's hand can trace,
And o'er the cheek of Sorrow throw
   A melancholy grace;
While Hope prolongs our happier hour,
Or deepest shades, that dimly lour
And blacken round our weary way,
Gilds with a gleam of distant day.

Still, where rosy Pleasure leads,
   See a kindred grief pursue;
Behind the steps that Misery treads,
   Approaching Comfort view:
The hues of bliss more brightly glow,
Chastised by sabler tints of woe;
And blended form, with artful strife,
The strength and harmony of life.

See the wretch, that long has tossed
   On the thorny bed of pain,
At length repair his vigour lost,
   And breathe and walk again:
The meanest floweret of the vale,
The simplest note that swells the gale,
The common sun, the air, and skies,
To him are opening Paradise.

HYMN TO IGNORANCE
A *Fragment*

Hail, horrors, hail! ye ever gloomy bowers,
Ye gothic fanes, and antiquated towers,
Where rushy Camus' slowly-winding flood
Perpetual draws his humid train of mud:
Glad I revisit thy neglected reign,
Oh take me to thy peaceful shade again.
But chiefly thee, whose influence breathed from high,
Augments the native darkness of the sky;
Ah, ignorance! soft salutary power!
Prostrate with filial reverence I adore.
Thrice hath Hyperion roll'd his annual race,
Since weeping I forsook thy fond embrace.
Oh say, successful dost thou still oppose
Thy leaden ægis 'gainst our ancient foes?
Still stretch, tenacious of thy right divine,
The massy sceptre o'er thy slumb'ring line?
And dews Lethean through the land dispense
To steep in slumbers each benighted sense?
If any spark of wit's delusive ray
Break out, and flash a momentary day,
With damp, cold touch forbid it to aspire,
And huddle up in fogs the dang'rous fire.
  Oh say – she hears me not, but, careless grown,
Lethargic nods upon her ebon throne.
Goddess! awake, arise! alas, my fears!
Can powers immortal feel the force of years?

Not thus of old, with ensigns wide unfurl'd,
She rode triumphant o'er the vanquish'd world;
Fierce Nations own'd her unresisted might,
And all was ignorance, and all was night.
   Oh! sacred age! Oh! times for ever lost!
(The schoolman's glory, and the churchman's boast.)
For ever gone – yet still to fancy new,
Her rapid wings the transient scene pursue,
And bring the buried ages back to view.
   High on her car, behold the grandam ride
Like old Sesostris with barbaric pride;
. . . a team of harness'd monarchs bend

*   *   *

EPITAPH ON MRS CLARKE

Lo! where this silent marble weeps,
A friend, a wife, a mother sleeps:
A heart, within whose sacred cell
The peaceful virtues lov'd to dwell.
Affection warm, and faith sincere,
And soft humanity were there.
In agony, in death resign'd,
She felt the wound she left behind,
Her infant image here below,
Sits smiling on a father's woe:
Whom what awaits, while yet he strays
Along the lonely vale of days?
A pang, to secret sorrow dear;
A sigh; an unavailing tear;
Till time shall every grief remove,
With life, with memory, and with love.

EPITAPH ON A CHILD

Here, free'd from pain, secure from misery, lies
A Child the Darling of his Parent's eyes:
A gentler Lamb ne'er sported on the plain,
A fairer Flower will never bloom again!
Few were the days allotted to his breath;
Here let him sleep in peace his night of death.

THE DESCENT OF ODIN

An Ode. From the Norse Tongue

Uprose the king of men with speed,
And saddled straight his coal-black steed;
Down the yawning steep he rode,
That leads to Hela's drear abode.
Him the dog of darkness spied;
His shaggy throat he open'd wide
(While from his jaws, with carnage fill'd,
Foam and human gore distill'd):
Hoarse he bays with hideous din,
Eyes that glow, and fangs that grin;
And long pursues with fruitless yell,
The father of the powerful spell.
Onward still his way he takes
(The groaning earth beneath him shakes),
Till full before his fearless eyes
The portals nine of hell arise.

Right against the eastern gate,
By the moss-grown pile he sate;
Where long of yore to sleep was laid
The dust of the prophetic maid.
Facing to the northern clime,
Thrice he trac'd the Runic rhyme;
Thrice pronounc'd, in accents dread,
The thrilling verse that wakes the dead:
Till from out the hollow ground
Slowly breath'd a sullen sound.

PROPHETESS

What call unknown, what charms presume
To break the quiet of the tomb?
Who thus afflicts my troubled sprite,
And drags me from the realms of night?
Long on these mould'ring bones have beat
The winter's snow, the summer's heat,
The drenching dews, and driving rain!
Let me, let me sleep again.
Who is he, with voice unblest,
That calls me from the bed of rest?

ODIN

A traveller, to thee unknown,
Is he that calls, a warrior's son.
Thou the deeds of light shalt know;
Tell me what is done below,
For whom yon glitt'ring board is spread,
Dress'd for whom yon golden bed?

PROPHETESS

Mantling in the goblet see
The pure bev'rage of the bee:
O'er it hangs the shield of gold;
'Tis the drink of Balder bold:
Balder's head to death is giv'n.
Pain can reach the sons of heav'n!
Unwilling I my lips unclose:
Leave me, leave me to repose.

ODIN

Once again my call obey,
Prophetess, arise, and say,
What dangers Odin's child await,
Who the author of his fate?

PROPHETESS

In Hoder's hand the hero's doom;
His brother sends him to the tomb.
Now my weary lips I close:
Leave me, leave me to repose.

ODIN

Prophetess, my spell obey,
Once again arise, and say,
Who th' avenger of his guilt,
By whom shall Hoder's blood be spilt?

PROPHETESS

In the caverns of the west,
By Odin's fierce embrace comprest,
A wond'rous boy shall Rinda bear,
Who ne'er shall comb his raven-hair,
Nor wash his visage in the stream,
Nor see the sun's departing beam,
Till he on Hoder's corse shall smile
Flaming on the fun'ral pile.
Now my weary lips I close:
Leave me, leave me to repose.

ODIN

Yet a while my call obey;
Prophetess, awake, and say,
What virgins these, in speechless woe,
That bend to earth their solemn brow,
That their flaxen tresses fear,
And snowy veils that float in air?
Tell me whence their sorrows rose:
Then I leave thee to repose.

PROPHETESS

Ha! no traveller art thou,
King of men, I know thee now;
Mightiest of a mighty line –

ODIN

No boding maid of skill divine
Art thou, nor prophetess of good;
But mother of the giant brood!

PROPHETESS

Hie thee hence, and boast at home,
That never shall enquirer come
To break my iron-sleep again;
Till Lok has burst his tenfold chain;
Never, till substantial night
Has reassum'd her ancient right;
Till wrapt in flames, in ruin hurl'd,
Sinks the fabric of the world.

STANZAS TO MR BENTLEY

In silent gaze the tuneful choir among,
    Half pleased, half blushing, let the Muse admire,
While Bentley leads her sister-art along,
    And bids the pencil answer to the lyre.

See, in their course, each transitory thought
    Fixed by his touch a lasting essence take;
Each dream, in fancy's airy colouring wrought
    To local symmetry and life awake!

The tardy rhymes that used to linger on,
    To censure cold, and negligent of fame,
In swifter measures animated run,
    And catch a lustre from his genuine flame.

Ah! could they catch his strength, his easy grace,
    His quick creation, his unerring line;
The energy of Pope they might efface,
    And Dryden's harmony submit to mine.

But not to one in this benighted age
    Is that diviner inspiration given,
That burns in Shakespeare's or in Milton's page,
    The pomp and prodigality of heaven.

As, when conspiring in the diamond's blaze,
    The meaner gems, that singly charm the sight,
Together dart their intermingled rays,
    And dazzle with a luxury of light.

Enough for me, if to some feeling breast
    My lines a secret sympathy [impart;]
And as their pleasing influence [flows confest,]
    A sigh of soft reflection [heaves the heart.]

SKETCH OF HIS OWN CHARACTER
Written in 1761, and Found in One of His Pocket-Books.

Too poor for a bribe, and too proud to importune;
He had not the method of making a fortune:
Could love, and could hate, so was thought somewhat
    odd;
No very great wit, he believ'd in a God:
A post or a pension he did not desire,
But left church and state to Charles Townshend and
    Squire.

WILLIAM SHAKESPEARE TO MRS ANNE, REGULAR SERVANT TO THE REVD MR PRECENTOR OF YORK

A moment's patience, gentle Mistris Anne!
(But stint your clack for sweet St Charitie)
'Tis Willy begs, once a right proper Man,
Tho' now a Book, and interleav'd, you see.

Much have I born from canker'd Critick's spite,
From fumbling Baronets, and Poets small,
Pert Barristers, & Parsons nothing bright:
But, what awaits me now, is worst of all!

'Tis true, our Master's temper natural
Was fashion'd fair in meek & dovelike guise:
But may not honey's self be turn'd to gall
By residence, by marriage, & sore eyes?

If then he wreak on me his wicked will:
Steal to his closet at the hour of prayer,
And (when thou hear'st the organ piping shrill)
Grease his best pen, & all he scribbles, tear.

Better to bottom tarts & cheesecakes nice,
Better the roast-meat from the fire to save,
Better be twisted into caps for spice,
Than thus be patch'd, & cobbled in one's grave!

So York shall taste, what Clouët never know;
So from *our* works sublimer fumes shall rise;
While Nancy earns the praise to Shakespear due
For glorious puddings, & immortal pies.

SONG

'Midst beauty and pleasure's gay triumphs, to languish
And droop without knowing the source of my
   anguish;
To start from short slumbers and look for the
   morning –
Yet close my dull eyes when I see it returning;

Sighs sudden and frequent, looks ever dejected,
Sounds that steal from my tongue, by no meaning
   connected!
Ah say, fellow-swains, how these symptoms befell me?
They smile, but reply not. Sure Delia will tell me!

ODE FOR MUSIC

I. AIR

'Hence, avaunt ('tis holy ground),
   Comus, and his midnight-crew,
And Ignorance with looks profound,
   And dreaming Sloth of pallid hue,
Mad Sedition's cry profane,
Servitude that hugs her chain,
Nor in these consecrated bowers,
Let painted Flatt'ry hide her serpent-train in flowers.

CHORUS

'Nor Envy base, nor creeping Gain,
Dare the Muse's walk to stain,
While bright-eyed Science watches round:
Hence, away, 'tis holy ground!'

II. RECITATIVE

From yonder realms of empyrean day
   Bursts on my ear th' indignant lay:
There sit the sainted sage, the bard divine,
   The few, whom genius gave to shine
Thro' every unborn age, and undiscover'd clime.
   Rapt in celestial transport they:
   Yet hither oft a glance from high
   They send of tender sympathy
To bless the place, where on their opening soul
   First the genuine ardour stole.

'Twas Milton struck the deep-ton'd shell,
And, as the choral warblings round him swell,
Meek Newton's self bends from his state sublime
And nods his hoary head, and listens to the rhyme.

III. AIR

'Ye brown o'er-arching groves,
    That contemplation loves,
Where willowy Camus lingers with delight!
    Oft at the blush of dawn
    I trod your level lawn,
Oft woo'd the gleam of Cynthia silver-bright
In cloisters dim, far from the haunts of Folly,
With Freedom by my side, and soft-eyed Melancholy.'

IV. RECITATIVE

But hark! the portals sound, and pacing forth
    With solemn steps and slow,
High potentates, and dames of royal birth,
And mitred fathers in long order go:
Great Edward, with the lilies on his brow
    From haughty Gallia torn,
And sad Chatillon, on her bridal morn
That wept her bleeding Love, and princely Clare,
And Anjou's heroine, and the paler rose,
The rival of her crown and of her woes,
    And either Henry there,
The murder'd saint, and the majestic lord,

That broke the bonds of Rome.
(Their tears, their little triumphs o'er,
   Their human passions no more,
Save Charity, that glows beyond the tomb.)

ACCOMPANIED

  All that on Granta's fruitful plain
  Rich streams of regal bounty pour'd,
And bad these awful fanes and turrets rise,
To hail their Fitzroy's festal morning come;
   And thus they speak in soft accord
   The liquid language of the skies:

V. QUARTETTO

'What is grandeur, what is power?
   Heavier toil, superior pain.
   What the bright reward we gain?
   The grateful memory of the good.
   Sweet is the breath of vernal shower,
   The bee's collected treasures sweet,
   Sweet music's melting fall, but sweeter yet
   The still small voice of gratitude.'

VI. RECITATIVE

Foremost and leaning from her golden cloud
   The venerable Marg'ret see!
'Welcome, my noble son (she cries aloud),
   To this, thy kindred train, and me:
Pleas'd in thy lineaments we trace
A Tudor's fire, a Beaufort's grace.

AIR

'Thy liberal heart, thy judging eye,
  The flow'r unheeded shall descry,
  And bid it round heav'n's altars shed
  The fragrance of its blushing head:
  Shall raise from earth the latent gem
  To glitter on the diadem.

VII. RECITATIVE

'Lo! Granta waits to lead her blooming band,
  Not obvious, not obtrusive, she
No vulgar praise, no venal incense flings;
  Nor dares with courtly tongue refin'd
Profane thy inborn royalty of mind:
  She reveres herself and thee.
With modest pride to grace thy youthful brow,
The laureate wreath, that Cecil wore, she brings,
  And to thy just, thy gentle hand,
  Submits the fasces of her sway,
While spirits blest above and men below
Join with glad voice the loud symphonious lay.

VIII. GRAND CHORUS

'Thro' the wild waves as they roar,
  With watchful eye and dauntless mien,
    Thy steady course of honour keep,
Nor fear the rocks, nor seek the shore:
  The star of Brunswick smiles serene,
    And gilds the horrors of the deep.'

THE FATAL SISTERS

An Ode. From the Norse Tongue

PREFACE

In the eleventh century Sigurd, Earl of the Orkney Islands, went
with a fleet of ships and a considerable body of troops into
Ireland, to the assistance of Sictryg with the silken beard, who
was then making war on his father-in-law Brian, King of Dublin:
the Earl and all his forces were cut to pieces, and Sictryg was in
danger of a total defeat; but the enemy had a greater loss by the
death of Brian, their King, who fell in the action. On Christmas-
day (the day of the battle), a native of Caithness in Scotland saw
at a distance a number of persons on horseback riding full speed
towards a hill, and seeming to enter into it. Curiosity led him to
follow them, till looking through an opening in the rocks he saw
twelve gigantic figures resembling women: they were all employed
about a loom; and as they wove, they sung the following
dreadful song; which when they had finished, they tore the web
into twelve pieces, and (each taking her portion) galloped six to
the north and as many to the south.

Now the storm begins to lower
   (Haste, the loom of hell prepare),
Iron sleet of arrowy shower
   Hurtles in the darken'd air.

Glitt'ring lances are the loom,
   Where the dusky warp we strain,
Weaving many a soldier's doom,
   Orkney's woe, and Randver's bane.

See the griesly texture grow!
   ('Tis of human entrails made)
And the weights, that play below,
   Each a gasping warrior's head.

Shafts for shuttles, dipt in gore,
   Shoot the trembling cords along.
Sword, that once a monarch bore,
   Keep the tissue close and strong.

Mista, black terrific maid,
   Sangrida, and Hilda, see,
Join the wayward work to aid:
   'Tis the woof of victory.

Ere the ruddy sun be set,
   Pikes must shiver, javelins sing,
Blade with clattering buckler meet,
   Hauberk crash, and helmet ring.

(Weave the crimson web of war)
   Let us go, and let us fly,
Where our friends the conflict share,
   Where they triumph, where they die.

As the paths of fate we tread,
   Wading through th' ensanguin'd field,
Gondula, and Geira, spread
   O'er the youthful king your shield.

We the reins to slaughter give,
   Ours to kill, and ours to spare:
Spite of danger he shall live.
   (Weave the crimson web of war.)

They, whom once the desert-beach
   Pent within its bleak domain,
Soon their ample sway shall stretch
   O'er the plenty of the plain.

Low the dauntless earl is laid,
   Gor'd with many a gaping wound:
Fate demands a nobler head;
   Soon a king shall bite the ground.

Long his loss shall Eirin weep,
   Ne'er again his likeness see;
Long her strains in sorrow steep:
   Strains of immortality!

Horror covers all the heath,
   Clouds of carnage blot the sun,
Sisters, weave the web of death;
   Sisters, cease; the work is done.

Hail the task, and hail the hands!
   Songs of joy and triumph sing!
Joy to the victorious bands;
   Triumph to the younger king.

Mortal, thou that hear'st the tale,
    Learn the tenour of our song.
Scotland, thro' each winding vale
    Far and wide the notes prolong.

Sisters, hence with spurs of speed:
    Each her thundering faulchion wield;
Each bestride her sable steed.
    Hurry, hurry to the field!

THE CANDIDATE

or, *The Cambridge Courtship*

When sly Jemmy Twitcher had smugg'd up his face,
With a lick of court white-wash, and pious grimace,
A wooing he went, where three sisters of old
In harmless society guttle and scold.

   'Lord! sister,' says Physic to Law, 'I declare
Such a sheep-biting look, such a pick-pocket air!
Not I for the Indies: – You know I'm no prude, –
But his nose is a shame, – and his eyes are so lewd!
Then he shambles and straddles so oddly – I fear –
No – at our time of life 'twould be silly, my dear.'

   'I don't know,' says Law, 'but methinks for his look,
'Tis just like the picture in Rochester's book;
Then his character, Phyzzy – his morals – his life –
When she died, I can't tell, but he once had a wife.
They say he's no Christian, loves drinking and w – g,
And all the town rings of his swearing and roaring!
His lying and filching, and Newgate-bird tricks; –
Not I – for a coronet, chariot and six.'

   Divinity heard, between waking and dozing,
Her sisters denying, and Jemmy proposing:
From table she rose, and with bumper in hand,
She strok'd up her belly, and strok'd down her band –
'What a pother is here about wenching and roaring!
Why, David lov'd catches, and Solomon w – g:
Did not Israel filch from th' Egyptians of old
Their jewels of silver and jewels of gold?

73

The prophet of Bethel, we read, told a lie:
He drinks – so did Noah; – he swears – so do I:
To reject him for such peccadillos, were odd;
Besides, he repents – for he talks about G** –
               [*To* Jemmy]
"Never hang down your head, you poor penitent elf,
Come buss me – I'll be Mrs Twitcher myself.'"
D-n ye both for a couple of Puritan bitches!
He's Christian enough, that repents, and that stitches.

THE TRIUMPHS OF OWEN
A Fragment. From the Welsh

Owen's praise demands my song,
Owen swift, and Owen strong;
Fairest flower of Roderic's stem,
Gwyneth's shield, and Britain's gem.
He nor heaps his brooded stores,
Nor on all profusely pours;
Lord of every regal art,
Liberal hand, and open heart.
Big with hosts of mighty name,
Squadrons three against him came;
This the force of Eirin hiding,
Side by side as proudly riding,
On her shadow long and gay
Lochlin plows the wat'ry way;
There the Norman sails afar
Catch the winds and join the war:
Black and huge along they sweep,
Burthens of the angry deep.

Dauntless on his native sands
The dragon-son of Mona stands;
In glitt'ring arms and glory drest,
High he rears his ruby crest.
There the thund'ring strokes begin,
There the press, and there the din;

Talymalfra's rocky shore
Echoing to the battle's roar.
Check'd by the torrent-tide of blood,
Backward Meinai rolls his flood;
While, heap'd his master's feet around,
Prostrate warriors gnaw the ground.
Where his glowing eye-balls turn,
Thousand banners round him burn:
Where he points his purple spear,
Hasty, hasty rout is there,
Marking with indignant eye
Fear to stop, and shame to fly.
There confusion, terror's child,
Conflict fierce and ruin wild,
Agony, that pants for breath,
Despair and honourable death.

IMPROMPTU

Suggested by a view, in 1766, of the seat and ruins of a deceased nobleman, at Kingsgate, Kent

Old, and abandon'd by each venal friend,
　Here Holland form'd the pious resolution
To smuggle a few years, and strive to mend
　A broken character and constitution.

On this congenial spot he fix'd his choice;
　Earl Goodwin trembled for his neighbouring sand;
Here sea-gulls scream, and cormorants rejoice,
　And mariners, though shipwreck'd, dread to land.

Here reign the blustering North and blighting East,
　No tree is heard to whisper, bird to sing;
Yet Nature could not furnish out the feast,
　Art he invokes new horrors still to bring.

Here mouldering fanes and battlements arise,
　Turrets and arches nodding to their fall,
Unpeopled monast'ries delude our eyes,
　And mimic desolation covers all.

'Ah!' said the sighing peer, 'had Bute been true,
　Nor Mungo's, Rigby's, Bradshaw's friendship vain,
Far better scenes than these had blest our view,
　And realis'd the beauties which we feign:

'Purg'd by the sword, and purified by fire,
    Then had we seen proud London's hated walls;
Owls would have hooted in St Peter's choir,
    And foxes stunk and litter'd in St Paul's.'

THE ALLIANCE OF EDUCATION AND GOVERNMENT

A Fragment

As sickly plants betray a niggard earth,
Whose barren bosom starves her generous birth,
Nor genial warmth, nor genial juice retains,
Their roots to feed, and fill their verdant veins:
And as in climes, where winter holds his reign,
The soil, though fertile, will not teem in vain,
Forbids her gems to swell, her shades to rise,
Nor trusts her blossoms to the churlish skies:
So draw mankind in vain the vital airs,
Unform'd, unfriended, by those kindly cares,
That health and vigour to the soul impart,
Spread the young thought, and warm the opening
    heart:
So fond instruction on the growing powers
Of nature idly lavishes her stores,
If equal justice with unclouded face
Smile not indulgent on the rising race,
And scatter with a free, though frugal hand,
Light golden showers of plenty o'er the land:
But tyranny has fix'd her empire there,
To check their tender hopes with chilling fear,
And blast the vernal promise of the year.

This spacious animated scene survey,
From where the rolling orb, that gives the day,
His sable sons with nearer course surrounds
To either pole, and life's remotest bounds,
How rude so e'er th' exterior form we find,
Howe'er opinion tinge the varied mind,
Alike to all, the kind, impartial heav'n
The sparks of truth and happiness has giv'n:
With sense to feel, with memory to retain,
They follow pleasure, and they fly from pain;
Their judgment mends the plan their fancy draws,
The event presages, and explores the cause;
The soft returns of gratitude they know,
By fraud elude, by force repel the foe;
While mutual wishes, mutual woes endear
The social smile, the sympathetic tear.

Say, then, through ages by what fate confin'd
To different climes seem different souls assign'd?
Here measur'd laws and philosophic ease
Fix, and improve the polish'd arts of peace;
There industry and gain their vigils keep,
Command the winds, and tame th' unwilling deep:
Here force and hardy deeds of blood prevail;
There languid pleasure sighs in every gale.
Oft o'er the trembling nations from afar
Has Scythia breath'd the living cloud of war;

And, where the deluge burst, with sweepy sway
Their arms, their kings, their gods were roll'd away.
As oft have issued, host impelling host,
The blue-eyed myriads from the Baltic coast,
The prostrate south to the destroyer yields
Her boasted titles, and her golden fields:
With grim delight the brood of winter view
A brighter day, and heav'ns of azure hue;
Scent the new fragrance of the breathing rose,
And quaff the pendant vintage as it grows.
Proud of the yoke, and pliant to the rod,
Why yet does Asia dread a monarch's nod,
While European freedom still withstands
Th' encroaching tide that drowns her lessening lands;
And sees far off, with an indignant groan,
Her native plains, and empires once her own?
Can opener skies and suns of fiercer flame
O'erpower the fire, that animates our frame;
As lamps, that shed at eve a cheerful ray,
Fade and expire beneath the eye of day?
Need we the influence of the northern star
To string our nerves and steel our hearts to war?
And, where the face of nature laughs around,
Must sick'ning virtue fly the tainted ground?

Unmanly thought! what seasons can control,
What fancied zone can circumscribe the soul,
Who, conscious of the source from whence she springs,
By reason's light, on resolution's wings,
Spite of her frail companion, dauntless goes
O'er Libya's deserts and through Zembla's snows?
She bids each slumb'ring energy awake,
Another touch, another temper take,
Suspends th' inferior laws that rule our clay:
The stubborn elements confess her sway;
Their little wants, their low desires, refine,
And raise the mortal to a height divine.

  Not but the human fabric from the birth
Imbibes a flavour of its parent earth:
As various tracts enforce a various toil,
The manners speak the idiom of their soil.
An iron-race the mountain-cliffs maintain,
Foes to the gentler genius of the plain:
For where unwearied sinews must be found
With side-long plough to quell the flinty ground,
To turn the torrent's swift-descending flood,
To brave the savage rushing from the wood,
What wonder if to patient valour train'd,
They guard with spirit, what by strength they gain'd?

And while their rocky ramparts round they see,
The rough abode of want and liberty,
(As lawless force from confidence will grow)
Insult the plenty of the vales below?
What wonder, in the sultry climes, that spread
Where Nile redundant o'er his summer-bed
From his broad bosom life and verdure flings,
And broods o'er Egypt with his wat'ry wings,
If with advent'rous oar and ready sail
The dusky people drive before the gale;
Or on frail floats to neighb'ring cities ride,
That rise and glitter o'er the ambient tide

*   *   *

EPITAPH ON SIR WILLIAM WILLIAMS

Here, foremost in the dangerous paths of fame,
   Young Williams fought for England's fair renown;
His mind each Muse, each Grace adorn'd his frame,
   Nor envy dar'd to view him with a frown.

At Aix, his voluntary sword he drew,
   There first in blood his infant honour seal'd;
From fortune, pleasure, science, love, he flew,
   And scorn'd repose when Britain took the field.

With eyes of flame, and cool undaunted breast,
   Victor he stood on Bellisle's rocky steeps –
Ah, gallant youth! this marble tells the rest,
   Where melancholy friendship bends, and weeps.

THE DEATH OF HOEL

Had I but the torrent's might,
With headlong rage and wild affright
Upon Deïra's squadrons hurled,
To rush and sweep them from the world!
   Too, too secure in youthful pride,
By them my friend, my Hoël, died,
Great Cian's son: of Madoc old
He asked no heaps of hoarded gold;
Alone in nature's wealth arrayed,
He asked and had the lovely maid.
   To Cattraeth's vale in glitt'ring row
Twice two hundred warriors go;
Every warrior's manly neck
Chains of regal honour deck,
Wreathed in many a golden link:
From the golden cup they drink
Nectar, that the bees produce,
Or the grape's ecstatic juice.
Flushed with mirth and hope they burn:
But none from Cattraeth's vale return,
Save Aeron brave and Conan strong
(Bursting through the bloody throng),
And I, the meanest of them all,
That live to weep and sing their fall.

AGRIPPINA
Fragment of a Tragedy

DRAMATIS PERSONÆ

AGRIPPINA, the Empress-mother.
NERO, the Emperor.
POPPÆA, believed to be in love with OTHO.
OTHO, a young man of quality, in love with POPPÆA.
SENECA, the Emperor's Preceptor.
ANICETUS, Captain of the Guards.
DEMETRIUS, the Cynic, friend to SENECA.
ACERONIA, Confidant to AGRIPPINA.

SCENE – *The Emperor's villa at Baiæ.*

Act I. SCENE I

AGRIPPINA. ACERONIA

AGRIP. 'Tis well, begone! your errand is perform'd,
                        [*Speaks as to* Anicetus *entering.*
The message needs no comment. Tell your master,
His mother shall obey him. Say you saw her
Yielding due reverence to his high command:
Alone, unguarded and without a lictor,
As fits the daughter of Germanicus.
Say, she retir'd to Antium; there to tend
Her household cares, a woman's best employment.

What if you add, how she turn'd pale and trembled:
You think you spied a tear stand in her eye,
And would have dropp'd, but that her pride restrain'd
    it?
(Go! you can paint it well) 'twill profit you,
And please the stripling. Yet 'twould dash his joy
To hear the spirit of Britannicus
Yet walks on earth: at least there are who know
Without a spell to raise, and bid it fire
A thousand haughty hearts, unus'd to shake
When a boy frowns, nor to be lured with smiles
To taste of hollow kindness, or partake
His hospitable board: they are aware
Of th' unpledg'd bowl, they love not aconite.

ACER. He's gone: and much I hope these walls
And the mute air are privy to your passion.
Forgive your servant's fears, who sees the danger alone
Which fierce resentment cannot fail to raise
In haughty youth, and irritated power.

AGRIP. And dost thou talk to me, to me of danger,
Of haughty youth and irritated power,
To her that gave it being, her that arm'd
This painted Jove, and taught his novice hand
To aim the forked bolt; while he stood trembling,
Scar'd at the sound, and dazzled with its brightness?

'Tis like, thou hast forgot, when yet a stranger
To adoration, to the grateful steam
Of flattery's incense, and obsequious vows
From voluntary realms, a puny boy,
Deck'd with no other lustre than the blood
Of Agrippina's race, he liv'd unknown
To fame, or fortune; haply eyed at distance
Some edileship, ambitious of the power
To judge of weights and measures; scarcely dar'd
On expectation's strongest wing to soar
High as the consulate, that empty shade
Of long-forgotten liberty: when I
Oped his young eye to bear the blaze of greatness;
Shew'd him where empire tower'd, and bade him
    strike
The noble quarry. Gods! then was the time
To shrink from danger; fear might then have worn
The mask of prudence; but a heart like mine,
A heart that glows with the pure Julian fire,
If bright ambition from her craggy seat
Display the radiant prize, will mount undaunted,
Gain the rough heights, and grasp the dangerous
    honour.

ACER. Through various life I have pursued your
    steps,
Have seen your soul, and wonder'd at its daring:

Hence rise my fears. Nor am I yet to learn
How vast the debt of gratitude which Nero
To such a mother owes; the world, you gave him,
Suffices not to pay the obligation.
  I well remember too (for I was present)
When in a secret and dead hour of night,
Due sacrifice perform'd with barb'rous rites
Of mutter'd charms, and solemn invocation,
You bade the Magi call the dreadful powers,
That read futurity, to know the fate
Impending o'er your son: their answer was,
If the son reign, the mother perishes.
Perish (you cried) the mother! reign the son!
He reigns, the rest is heav'n's; who oft has bade,
Ev'n when its will seem'd wrote in lines of blood,
Th' unthought event disclose a whiter meaning.
Think too how oft in weak and sickly minds
The sweets of kindness lavishly indulg'd
Rankle to gall; and benefits too great
To be repaid, sit heavy on the soul,
As unrequited wrongs. The willing homage
Of prostrate Rome, the senate's joint applause,
The riches of the earth, the train of pleasures
That wait on youth, and arbitrary sway:
These were your gift, and with them you bestow'd
The very power he has to be ungrateful.

AGRIP. Thus ever grave and undisturb'd reflection
Pours its cool dictates in the madding ear
Of rage, and thinks to quench the fire it feels not.
Say'st thou I must be cautious, must be silent,
And tremble at the phantom I have raised?
Carry to him thy timid counsels. He
Perchance may heed 'em: tell him too, that one
Who had such liberal power to give, may still
With equal power resume that gift, and raise
A tempest that shall shake her own creation
To its original atoms – tell me! say
This mighty emperor, this dreaded hero,
Has he beheld the glittering front of war?
Knows his soft ear the trumpet's thrilling voice,
And outcry of the battle? Have his limbs
Sweat under iron harness? Is he not
The silken son of dalliance, nurs'd in ease
And pleasure's flow'ry lap? Rubellius lives,
And Sylla has his friends, though school'd by fear
To bow the supple knee, and court the times
With shows of fair obeisance; and a call,
Like mine, might serve belike to wake pretensions
Drowsier than theirs, who boast the genuine blood
Of our imperial house.

ACER. Did I not wish to check this dangerous
passion,

I might remind my mistress that her nod
Can rouse eight hardy legions, wont to stem
With stubborn nerves the tide, and face the rigour
Of bleak Germania's snows. Four, not less brave,
That in Armenia quell the Parthian force
Under the warlike Corbulo, by you
Mark'd for their leader: these, by ties confirm'd,
Of old respect and gratitude, are yours.
Surely the Masians too, and those of Egypt,
Have not forgot your sire: the eye of Rome,
And the Prætorian camp have long rever'd
With custom'd awe, the daughter, sister, wife,
And mother of their Cæsars.

   AGRIP.   Ha! by Juno,
It bears a noble semblance. On this base
My great revenge shall rise; or say we sound
The trump of liberty; there will not want,
Even in the servile senate, ears to own
Her spirit-stirring voice; Soranus there,
And Cassius; Vetus too, and Thrasea,
Minds of the antique cast, rough, stubborn souls,
That struggle with the yoke. How shall the spark
Unquenchable, that glows within their breasts,
Blaze into freedom, when the idle herd
(Slaves from the womb, created but to stare,
And bellow in the Circus) yet will start,

And shake 'em at the name of liberty,
Stung by a senseless word, a vain tradition,
As there were magic in it? Wrinkled beldams
Teach it their grandchildren, as somewhat rare
That anciently appear'd, but when, extends
Beyond their chronicle – oh! 'tis a cause
To arm the hand of childhood, and rebrace
The slacken'd sinews of time-wearied age.

    Yes, we may meet, ungrateful boy, we may!
Again the buried Genius of old Rome
Shall from the dust uprear his reverend head,
Rous'd by the shout of millions: there before
His high tribunal thou and I appear.
Let majesty sit on thy awful brow,
And lighten from thy eye: around thee call
The gilded swarm that wantons in the sunshine
Of thy full favour; Seneca be there
In gorgeous phrase of labour'd eloquence
To dress thy plea, and Burrhus strengthen it
With his plain soldier's oath, and honest seeming.
Against thee, liberty and Agrippina:
The world, the prize; and fair befall the victors.

    But soft! why do I waste the fruitless hours
In threats unexecuted? Haste thee, fly
These hated walls that seme to mock my shame,
And cast me forth in duty to their lord.

ACER. 'Tis time to go, the sun is high advanc'd,
And, ere mid-day, Nero will come to Baiæ.

AGRIP. My thought aches at him; not the basilisk
More deadly to the sight, than is to me
The cool injurious eye of frozen kindness.
I will not meet its poison. Let him feel
Before he sees me.

ACER.   Why then stays my sovereign,
Where he so soon may –

AGRIP.   Yes, I will be gone,
But not to Antium – all shall be confess'd,
Whate'er the frivolous tongue of giddy fame
Has spread among the crowd; things, that but
      whisper'd
Have arch'd the hearer's brow, and riveted
His eyes in fearful extasy: no matter
What; so't be strange, and dreadful. – Sorceries,
Assassinations, poisonings – the deeper
My guilt, the blacker his ingratitude.
      And you, ye manes of ambition's victims,
Enshrined Claudius, with the pitied ghosts
Of the Syllani, doom'd to early death,
(Ye unavailing horrors, fruitless crimes!)
If from the realms of night my voice ye hear,

In lieu of penitence, and vain remorse,
Accept my vengeance. Though by me ye bled,
He was the cause. My love, my fears for him,
Dried the soft springs of pity in my heart,
And froze them up with deadly cruelty.
Yet if your injur'd shades demand my fate,
If murder cries for murder, blood for blood,
Let me not fall alone; but crush his pride,
And sink the traitor in his mother's ruin.   [*Exeunt.*

SCENE II. OTHO, POPPÆA

OTHO. Thus far we're safe. Thanks to the rosy queen
Of amorous thefts: and had her wanton son
Lent us his wings, we could not have beguil'd
With more elusive speed the dazzled sight
Of wakeful jealousy. Be gay securely;
Dispel, my fair, with smiles, the tim'rous cloud
That hangs on thy clear brow. So Helen look'd,
So her white neck reclin'd, so was she borne
By the young Trojan to his gilded bark
With fond reluctance, yielding modesty,
And oft reverted eye, as if she knew not
Whether she fear'd, or wish'd to be pursued.

*   *   *